YOUR COMPLETE
PISCES 2024
PERSONAL
HOROSCOPE

Monthly Astrological Prediction Forecast Readings of
Every Zodiac Astrology Sun Star Signs- Love,
Romance, Money, Finances, Career, Health, Travel,
Spirituality.

Iris Quinn

Alpha Zuriel Publishing

Your Complete Pisces 2024 Personal Horoscope/ Iris Quinn. -- 1st ed.

"In the dance of the planets, we find the rhythms of life. Astrology reminds us that we are all connected to the greater universe, and our actions have ripple effects throughout the cosmos."

— IRIS QUINN

CONTENTS

CHAPTER ONE

PISCES PROFILE

- Constellation: Pisces
- Zodiac symbol: Fish
- Date: February 19 – March 20
- Element: Water
- Ruling Planet: Neptune
- Career Planet: Jupiter
- Love Planet: Venus
- Money Planet: Jupiter
- Planet of Fun, Entertainment, Creativity, and Speculations: Neptune
- Planet of Health and Work: Mercury
- Planet of Home and Family Life: Moon
- Planet of Spirituality: Neptune
- Planet of Travel, Education, Religion, and Philosophy: Jupiter

Colors:
- Colors: Sea Green, Aqua Blue

- Colors that promote love, romance, and social harmony: Lavender, Soft Pink
- Color that promotes earning power: Silver

Gem: Aquamarine
Metals: Tin
Scent: Sea Breeze
Birthstone: Aquamarine

Qualities:
• Quality: Mutable (represents adaptability)
• Quality most needed for balance: Practicality

Strongest Virtues:
• Compassion
• Sensitivity
• Imagination
• Creativity
• Intuition

Deepest Need: Emotional connection and understanding.

Characteristics to Avoid:
• Escapism
• Overindulgence
• Being overly idealistic
• Self-pity

Signs of Greatest Overall Compatibility:
• Cancer
• Scorpio

Signs of Greatest Overall Incompatibility:
• Gemini
• Virgo
• Sagittarius

- Sign Most Supportive for Career Advancement: Capricorn
- Sign Most Supportive for Emotional Well-being: Cancer
- Sign Most Supportive Financially: Taurus
- Sign Best for Marriage and/or Partnerships: Libra
- Sign Most Supportive for Creative Projects: Leo
- Best Sign to Have Fun With: Leo

Signs Most Supportive in Spiritual Matters:
• Scorpio
• Pisces

Best Day of the Week: Thursday

PISCES TRAITS

- Compassionate and empathetic nature
- Tendency to be overly emotional and moody.
- Highly intuitive and sensitive
- Escapist tendencies and difficulty facing reality.
- Creative and imaginative
- Indecisiveness and difficulty making firm decisions.
- Selfless and willing to help others.

PERSONALITY OF PISCES

The personality of Pisces is characterized by their deep emotional nature, compassion, and artistic inclination. Pisces individuals are known for their empathetic and intuitive abilities, often being able to understand and connect with others on a deep emotional level. They have a strong sense of empathy and are highly sensitive to the feelings and needs of those around them.

Pisces is a water sign, which contributes to their emotional depth and sensitivity. They are imaginative and creative, often having a strong artistic or imaginative streak. Many Pisces individuals excel in fields such as art, music, writing, or other creative endeavors.

Pisces individuals are known for their selflessness and willingness to help others. They have a natural inclination to be of service and are often drawn to charitable or humanitarian causes. They are compassionate and caring, always seeking to support and uplift those in need.

On the flip side, Pisces can sometimes struggle with boundaries and may have a tendency to absorb the emotions of others, which can lead to emotional overwhelm. They may also be prone to escapism or avoidance of harsh realities, preferring to retreat into their own imaginative world.

Pisces individuals are often deeply connected to their spiritual side and may have a strong sense of intuition or psychic abilities. They are open-minded and may have an interest in exploring mystical or metaphysical subjects.

Overall, the personality of Pisces is one that is sensitive, compassionate, imaginative, and spiritually attuned. They have a natural ability to connect with others and bring a sense of empathy and understanding to their relationships and interactions.

WEAKNESSES OF PISCES

Pisces individuals, while possessing many strengths, also have certain weaknesses that they may need to navigate in their lives:

In their quest to navigate the depths of their emotions and the vast ocean of possibilities, Pisces individuals can sometimes find themselves overwhelmed by their own sensitivities. Their highly empathetic nature can make it challenging for them to maintain healthy emotional boundaries, leading to moments of emotional turbulence.

At times, Pisces individuals may struggle with the need to escape from the harsh realities of life. This desire for retreat can manifest as a tendency to daydream, seek solace in fantasies, or even turn to unhealthy coping mechanisms. While this escapism may provide temporary respite, it can also hinder their ability to confront and address real-world challenges.

Pisces individuals can find decision-making to be a complex task. Their compassionate and understanding nature often leads them to consider multiple perspectives, making it difficult for them to settle on a definitive choice. They may become caught in a cycle of overthinking and hesitation, fearing that their decisions may have unintended consequences.

Additionally, the trusting nature of Pisces individuals can sometimes leave them vulnerable to being taken advantage of or deceived. Their inclination to see the best in others and give people the benefit of the doubt can lead to disappointments and heartaches if they encounter individuals who do not reciprocate their sincerity.

Understanding these weaknesses allows Pisces individuals to navigate their lives with awareness and work towards finding a healthy balance between their strengths and areas of growth.

RELATIONSHIP COMPATIBILITY WITH PISCES

Based only on their Sun signs, this is how Pisces interacts with others. These are the compatibility interpretations for all 12 potential Pisces combinations. This is a limited and insufficient method of determining compatibility.

However, Sun-sign compatibility remains the foundation for overall harmony in a relationship.

The general rule is that yin and yang do not get along. Yin complements yin, and yang complements yang. While yin and yang partnerships can be successful, they require more effort. Earth and water zodiac signs are both Yin. Yang is represented by the fire and air zodiac signs.

Pisces (Yin) and Aries (Yang):

When a Pisces individual enters into a relationship with an Aries individual, their contrasting Yin and Yang energies create an intriguing dynamic. Pisces brings a sensitive and intuitive nature, while Aries

9

brings a fiery and passionate energy. This combination can lead to a relationship filled with both depth and excitement.

Pisces and Aries can complement each other well. Pisces appreciates the boldness and assertiveness of Aries, while Aries admires the compassion and empathy of Pisces. They can inspire each other to explore new adventures and support one another's personal growth.

However, challenges may arise due to their differing approaches to life. Pisces may feel overwhelmed by the intensity and impulsiveness of Aries, while Aries may struggle to understand Pisces' emotional depth. Communication and understanding are key to navigating these differences and finding a harmonious balance in the relationship.

Pisces (Yin) and Taurus (Yin):

When Pisces joins forces with Taurus, their shared Yin energy creates a deep sense of emotional connection and stability. Both signs value comfort, loyalty, and security in a relationship. They appreciate the beauty of life and enjoy creating a serene and harmonious home environment together.

Pisces' dreamy and imaginative nature blends well with Taurus' practicality and grounding presence. Taurus provides a sense of stability that Pisces craves, while Pisces brings creativity and emotional depth to the relationship. Together, they can build a strong and enduring partnership based on trust and mutual support.

However, conflicts may arise due to their different ways of handling emotions. Pisces may be more sensitive and prone to mood swings, while Taurus can be stubborn and resistant to change. Open communication and willingness to compromise are essential for maintaining a healthy and fulfilling relationship.

Pisces (Yin) and Gemini (Yang):

When Pisces connects with Gemini, their contrasting Yin and Yang energies create a relationship that is both dynamic and complex. Pisces brings depth, sensitivity, and intuition, while Gemini brings versatility, intellectual curiosity, and sociability.

Pisces and Gemini can learn from each other's strengths and broaden their horizons through shared experiences. Pisces can help Gemini tap into their emotions and navigate the realm of intuition, while

Gemini can bring a sense of intellectual stimulation and playfulness to Pisces' life.

However, challenges may arise due to their different approaches to communication and commitment. Pisces may seek emotional depth and security, while Gemini may be more inclined to keep things light and maintain a sense of freedom. Finding a balance between emotional connection and individuality is crucial for the success of their relationship.

Pisces (Yin) and Cancer (Yin):

When Pisces and Cancer come together, their shared Yin energy creates a deeply nurturing and emotionally supportive relationship. Both signs are highly intuitive, empathetic, and value emotional connection. They understand and appreciate each other's needs, creating a strong bond built on trust and understanding.

Pisces and Cancer share a love for creating a loving and harmonious home environment. They can build a sanctuary of emotional security and find comfort in each other's presence. Their shared sensitivity and empathy enable them to provide emotional support during challenging times.

However, both signs may struggle with setting boundaries and may be prone to mood swings. It is important for Pisces and Cancer to communicate openly and honestly to avoid being overwhelmed by emotions. By nurturing their emotional connection and supporting each other's growth, they can create a deeply fulfilling and long-lasting partnership.

Pisces (Yin) and Leo (Yang):

When Pisces and Leo come together, their contrasting Yin and Yang energies create a relationship filled with both depth and excitement. Pisces brings a sensitive and intuitive nature, while Leo exudes confidence, passion, and a charismatic presence.

Pisces is drawn to Leo's warmth and generosity, while Leo is captivated by Pisces' mysterious and compassionate nature. They can inspire each other to embrace creativity and pursue their passions. Pisces brings emotional depth and understanding to Leo's life, while Leo provides Pisces with a sense of security and admiration.

However, conflicts may arise due to their differing needs for attention and recognition. Leo may desire the spotlight, while Pisces may prefer a more behind-the-scenes role. Balancing individual needs with shared aspirations is essential for their relationship to thrive.

Pisces (Yin) and Virgo (Yang):

When Pisces connects with Virgo, their contrasting Yin and Yang energies create a complementary partnership. Pisces brings emotional depth, intuition, and creativity, while Virgo contributes practicality, organization, and attention to detail.

Pisces is attracted to Virgo's grounded nature and stability, while Virgo admires Pisces' artistic and imaginative spirit. They can learn from each other, with Pisces encouraging Virgo to embrace their emotions and Virgo helping Pisces bring their dreams into practical reality.

However, challenges may arise due to their different approaches to life and decision-making. Pisces may be more inclined to go with the flow, while Virgo seeks structure and order. Finding a middle ground between flexibility and practicality is crucial for their relationship to flourish.

Pisces (Yin) and Libra (Yang):

When Pisces and Libra come together, their contrasting Yin and Yang energies create a harmonious and balanced partnership. Pisces brings sensitivity, empathy, and an appreciation for beauty, while Libra contributes diplomacy, charm, and a desire for harmony.

Pisces and Libra share a love for art, culture, and intellectual pursuits. They can engage in deep and meaningful conversations, appreciating each other's perspectives and fostering a sense of mutual respect. Their connection is built on a strong emotional and intellectual bond.

However, conflicts may arise due to their different approaches to decision-making and conflict resolution. Pisces may be more inclined to avoid confrontation, while Libra seeks fairness and balance. Effective communication and compromise are essential for maintaining a harmonious and fulfilling relationship.

Pisces (Yin) and Scorpio (Yin):

When Pisces and Scorpio come together, their shared Yin energy creates a relationship that is intense, passionate, and emotionally transformative. Both signs are highly intuitive, perceptive, and deeply connected to their emotions.

Pisces and Scorpio understand each other on a profound level and share a powerful emotional bond. They can navigate the depths of their emotions together and support each other through life's challenges. Their connection is characterized by loyalty, trust, and a shared desire for emotional growth.

However, their intense emotional nature may lead to occasional power struggles and moments of jealousy. It is important for Pisces and Scorpio to foster open and honest communication, allowing for mutual understanding and the resolution of conflicts. By embracing vulnerability and emotional authenticity, they can cultivate a relationship filled with deep intimacy and mutual support.

Pisces (Yin) and Sagittarius (Yang):

When Pisces and Sagittarius come together, their contrasting Yin and Yang energies create a relationship that is both adventurous and spiritually enlightening. Pisces brings sensitivity, intuition, and emotional depth, while Sagittarius adds enthusiasm, optimism, and a love for exploration.

Pisces and Sagittarius can inspire each other to expand their horizons, both intellectually and spiritually. Pisces admires Sagittarius' adventurous spirit, while Sagittarius appreciates Pisces' compassion and ability to see beyond the surface. They can embark on exciting journeys together and explore the realms of both the physical and the metaphysical.

However, conflicts may arise due to their differing needs for security and freedom. Pisces may desire emotional security and stability, while Sagittarius craves independence and spontaneity. Finding a balance between individual freedom and shared commitments is crucial for the success of their relationship.

Pisces (Yin) and Capricorn (Yin):

When Pisces joins forces with Capricorn, their shared Yin energy creates a relationship that is both nurturing and practical. Pisces brings emotional depth, empathy, and imagination, while Capricorn adds stability, ambition, and a strong sense of responsibility.

Pisces finds comfort and security in Capricorn's grounded nature, while Capricorn appreciates Pisces' compassion and sensitivity. They can create a stable and supportive foundation for their relationship, combining Pisces' emotional depth with Capricorn's determination and practicality.

However, conflicts may arise due to their different approaches to life and priorities. Pisces may be more inclined to go with the flow and follow their intuition, while Capricorn is driven by goals and long-term plans. Finding a balance between spontaneity and structure is key to maintaining a harmonious and fulfilling partnership.

Pisces (Yin) and Aquarius (Yang):

When Pisces connects with Aquarius, their contrasting Yin and Yang energies create a unique and intellectually stimulating relationship. Pisces brings emotional depth, intuition, and a dreamy nature, while Aquarius contributes innovation, intellectual curiosity, and a love for social connections.

Pisces and Aquarius can learn from each other and bring out the best in one another. Pisces helps Aquarius tap into their emotions and infuse empathy into their endeavors, while Aquarius encourages Pisces to embrace their individuality and think outside the box.

However, challenges may arise due to their different approaches to emotions and personal boundaries. Pisces may be more sensitive and prone to mood swings, while Aquarius tends to be more detached and focused on intellectual pursuits. Building open and honest communication, as well as respecting each other's unique qualities, is essential for their relationship to thrive.

Pisces (Yin) and Pisces (Yin):

When two Pisces individuals come together, their shared Yin energy creates a relationship that is deeply compassionate, emotionally connected, and spiritually attuned. They understand each other's emotional complexities and share a profound level of empathy.

Pisces and Pisces can create a safe and nurturing space where they can express themselves fully and explore their dreams and aspirations. They have a natural understanding of each other's needs and can provide emotional support during both the highs and lows of life.

However, challenges may arise due to their shared sensitivities and emotional nature. Both individuals may need to work on setting boundaries and maintaining their individuality within the relationship. It is important for them to cultivate open communication and balance their emotional depths with practical considerations.

Overall, Pisces individuals can find compatibility with a range of zodiac signs. However, the success of their relationships will depend on their ability to communicate, understand each other's needs, and embrace the unique dynamics that each pairing brings.

LOVE AND PASSION

Love and passion are deeply intertwined in the world of Pisces. As a water sign ruled by Neptune, Pisces is known for their romantic and dreamy nature. Love is an essential aspect of their lives, and they approach relationships with an open heart and a desire for profound emotional connections.

Pisces individuals are incredibly intuitive and empathetic, making them highly attuned to their partner's needs and emotions. They have a natural ability to understand and support their loved ones, often acting as a source of comfort and solace. Their compassionate nature allows them to create a safe and nurturing space where love can flourish.

When Pisces falls in love, they dive headfirst into a world of passion and devotion. They are incredibly romantic, often indulging in grand gestures and poetic expressions of love. They are not afraid to wear their heart on their sleeve and shower their partner with affection.

Pisces individuals seek a deep and spiritual connection with their partner. They crave emotional intimacy and are drawn to partners who can match their level of depth and vulnerability. Trust and understanding are paramount in a Pisces' love life, as they long for a soulful bond that transcends the superficial.

In relationships, Pisces can be incredibly selfless and giving. They are willing to go to great lengths to make their partner happy and will prioritize their loved one's needs above their own. However, they also have a tendency to lose themselves in the process, sometimes sacrificing their own desires and boundaries.

Pisces' passion stems from their ability to tap into their emotions and unleash their creative and imaginative side. They approach love with a sense of fantasy and idealism, viewing their partner through a lens of romance and enchantment. Their love language often involves acts of kindness, heartfelt gestures, and an unwavering devotion to their significant other.

At times, Pisces' intense emotions and sensitivity can make them vulnerable to heartbreak. They can easily get caught up in illusions or idealized versions of their partner, leading to disappointment when reality falls short. It is important for Pisces to find a partner who appreciates their emotional nature and reciprocates their love and devotion.

In summary, love and passion are essential elements in the life of a Pisces. Their romantic and dreamy nature, coupled with their deep empathy and sensitivity, allows them to create profound connections with their partners. When love blossoms for a Pisces, it becomes a transformative and all-encompassing experience filled with tenderness, romance, and a spiritual connection that transcends the ordinary.

MARRIAGE

MARRIAGE is an important aspect of life for Pisces individuals. They are generally supportive of the institution of marriage and value the emotional security and stability it can provide. However, before committing to marriage, Pisces often feel the need to ensure their financial position is stable, as they desire a sense of security for themselves and their future family.

In a marriage, Pisces must be mindful of their predisposition to engage in disputes and criticize their partner. While their intentions may be well-meaning, excessive criticism can weaken their partner's morale and jeopardize the harmony of the relationship. It is essential for Pisces to cultivate open and honest communication, expressing their concerns and needs in a compassionate and constructive manner.

Pisces individuals strive like no one else to keep their marriage alive. They are deeply committed to their partners and are willing to put in the effort to make the relationship work. However, if they believe that the disagreements and challenges in the marriage are insurmountable, they will not hesitate to consider ending the relationship in order to prioritize their emotional well-being.

When it comes to balancing work and family duties, Pisces can benefit from the support and adaptability of a partner like Virgo women. Virgo women understand the importance of order and efficiency in the marriage, and they approach their marital tasks with a diligent and positive attitude. They excel in managing the practical aspects of family life, providing a sense of stability and structure that complements Pisces' emotional nature.

Similarly, Virgo males are dedicated workers who value their roles as parents and husbands. They actively participate in household responsibilities and are committed to creating a harmonious and nurturing environment for their family. They are not sexist and believe in equal partnership, ensuring that their spouse is never burdened with more than their fair share of responsibilities.

Marriage holds great significance for Pisces individuals. They approach it with a desire for emotional security and strive to maintain a harmonious and fulfilling relationship. By addressing financial stability, tempering disputes, and seeking compatibility with partners who understand their emotional nature, Pisces can create a loving and supportive marriage that allows them to thrive personally and as a couple.

CHAPTER TWO

PISCES 2024 HOROSCOPE

Overview Pisces 2024

Dear Pisces, as you step into the year 2024, the cosmos is aligning in a way that will shape your journey in profound ways. The planetary movements throughout the year indicate a time of opportunities, challenges, and growth. The alignment of Mercury, Uranus, Sun, Venus, Mars, Jupiter, Saturn, Neptune, Chiron, and Pluto will play a crucial role in various aspects of your life, including your career, relationships, health, and personal development.

The year begins with Mercury in Taurus forming a semi-square with Neptune in Pisces in late May,

27

suggesting a period of potential confusion or misunderstanding at work. It's important to communicate clearly and honestly during this time and to seek clarity when needed. The Sun in Gemini forming a semi-square with Chiron in Aries in late May also suggests that healing and recovery may be themes in your professional life at this time.

In June, Mercury in Taurus forms a sextile with Saturn in Pisces, indicating a period of stability and potential growth in your financial situation. This is a good time to invest or save money. However, the square between Venus and Uranus in August suggests potential unexpected expenses or financial changes. It's important to be prepared for these potential fluctuations and to manage your finances wisely.

In terms of relationships and social life, the square between Venus and Neptune in June indicates a time of confusion or misunderstanding in your relationships. It's important to communicate clearly and honestly during this time and to seek clarity when needed. The sextile between Mercury and the True Node in June also suggests that communication and social interactions will be particularly important during this time. This is a good time to build and strengthen relationships.

As the year progresses, you will find that your social life picks up pace. There is a sense of camaraderie and belonging that envelops you. Engage in social activities, but be mindful of not overcommitting yourself. Balance is key.

Your health and wellness are areas that require attention this year. The sesquiquadrate between the Sun and Chiron in June is a call for healing. This is the time to integrate wellness practices into your daily routine. Whether it's through yoga, meditation, or simply spending time in nature, nurturing your well-being is essential.

The latter part of the year brings vitality. The sextile between the Sun and Chiron in June is a rejuvenating energy. Engage in physical activities that not only strengthen your body but also bring joy to your soul.

On a spiritual level, 2024 is a year of profound growth and learning. The quintile between Jupiter and Saturn in May is a cosmic classroom. This is a time of spiritual learning and seeking higher wisdom. You are being called to delve deeper into the mysteries of life.

The conjunction between Venus and Pluto in July is a catalyst for transformation. This is a period of shedding old skins and emerging anew. Embrace the changes and allow yourself to grow and evolve.

Overall, Pisces, the year 2024 will be a year of growth, transformation, and self-discovery. While there will be challenges along the way, these challenges will provide opportunities for personal development and understanding. Embrace the journey and make the most of the opportunities that come your way. Stay open to learning and growing, and don't be afraid to explore new paths. Your adventurous spirit will guide you through the ups and downs of the year, leading you to new heights in your personal and professional life.

January 2024

Horoscope

January 2024 presents a dynamic mix of energies for Pisces individuals. The month begins with a challenging aspect as Venus squares Saturn on January 1st. This aspect may bring forth obstacles and a sense of restriction, particularly in your personal relationships or financial matters. You may feel a lack of harmony and find it challenging to express your emotions. It's important to approach these challenges with patience and a resilient mindset. This aspect urges you to reevaluate your commitments and make necessary adjustments to find a balance. Use this time to reflect on your values and priorities.

However, as the month progresses, several positive aspects offer support and opportunities for growth. On January 3rd, Mercury quintiles Saturn, enhancing your mental clarity and communication skills. This alignment enables you to express yourself with precision and authenticity. Your ideas and thoughts carry weight, making it an opportune time to engage in

31

meaningful conversations, negotiations, or important discussions. Use your enhanced communication abilities to build solid connections with others.

Love

In January 2024, the realm of love and relationships for Pisces individuals may experience fluctuations. The quincunx aspect between Venus and Jupiter on January 3rd signifies the need for adjustments and compromises in your romantic partnerships. This aspect challenges you to find a harmonious balance between your personal desires and the needs of your partner. It's crucial to communicate openly and honestly, seeking understanding and cooperation. Be patient and willing to make compromises to maintain the harmony in your relationships.

Despite these initial challenges, a trine aspect between Venus and Chiron on January 11th brings emotional healing and deeper connections in your relationships. This period presents an opportunity to address past wounds, nurture emotional intimacy, and foster a stronger bond with your loved ones. It's a time to practice empathy, compassion, and forgiveness. By embracing vulnerability and open-heartedness, you can create a more profound sense of connection and understanding with your partner.

Single Pisces individuals may also find this period favorable for self-discovery and healing. Embrace self-love and self-care practices to build a strong foundation for future relationships. Engage in activities that bring you joy and allow you to express your authentic self. Use this time to clarify your desires and intentions for future romantic endeavors.

Career

January 2024 holds promising opportunities for career growth and advancement for Pisces individuals. The trine aspect between Mars and Jupiter on January 12th ignites your motivation, ambition, and professional success. This alignment fuels your drive to achieve your goals, take calculated risks, and embrace new opportunities. Your assertiveness and confidence will be noticed by superiors and colleagues, leading to positive recognition and career advancements. Trust your abilities and seize the moment to make significant strides in your professional journey.

Additionally, the sextile aspect between Mercury and Saturn on January 18th enhances your focus, organizational skills, and attention to detail. This alignment supports your ability to plan effectively, set realistic goals, and make long-term commitments. It's an excellent time to engage in strategic thinking, establish professional relationships, or seek guidance from mentors or experts in your field. Use your analytical skills to analyze your current career trajectory and identify areas for growth and improvement. This aspect encourages you to take practical steps towards achieving your long-term career objectives.

Finance

Financial matters in January 2024 require careful consideration and prudent decision-making for Pisces individuals. The semi-square aspect between Venus and Pluto on January 10th suggests the need for financial caution. It's crucial to be mindful of your expenditures, avoid impulsive purchases, and focus on long-term financial stability. This aspect reminds you of the importance of saving and budgeting wisely. Evaluate your financial goals and adjust your spending habits accordingly. Seek opportunities to reduce unnecessary expenses and consider long-term investments that align with your financial aspirations.

However, the biquintile aspect between Venus and Uranus on January 19th brings unexpected opportunities for financial gains. This alignment encourages you to stay open to new ideas, embrace innovation, and be willing to take calculated risks. It's a favorable time to explore alternative income sources, consider investment options, or embark on entrepreneurial ventures. However, it's essential to conduct thorough research and seek professional advice before making any significant financial decisions. Trust your intuition and make informed choices based on a solid understanding of the potential risks and rewards.

Remember to maintain a balanced approach to your finances, finding harmony between practicality and embracing new opportunities. Cultivate an abundance mindset and remain open to unexpected financial blessings. With careful planning and wise decision-making, you can achieve stability and grow your wealth in the long run.

Health

Pisces individuals need to prioritize their physical and emotional well-being in January 2024. The square aspect between the Sun and Chiron on January 6th highlights the importance of self-care and addressing any lingering health concerns. This alignment encourages you to pay attention to your body's signals and seek appropriate medical care or holistic therapies as needed. It's crucial to listen to your physical and emotional needs, as neglecting them can hinder your overall well-being. Take time to rest, recharge, and indulge in activities that nourish your mind, body, and soul.

The sextile aspect between the Sun and Neptune on January 15th fosters spiritual and emotional healing. Engage in activities that bring you a sense of peace and tranquility. Meditation, yoga, spending time in nature, or pursuing creative outlets can help you maintain a healthy balance between your inner and outer world. This period provides an opportunity to deepen your connection with your inner self and tap into your intuition. By prioritizing your emotional well-being, you can navigate the challenges of daily life with greater resilience and grace.

Additionally, ensure you have a support system in place. Reach out to loved ones, friends, or professionals who can provide guidance and assistance if you're facing any health challenges. It's important to seek help and not hesitate to ask for support when needed. Remember that self-care is an ongoing practice, and small, consistent efforts can have a significant impact on your overall health and vitality.

Travel

Travel opportunities may arise for Pisces in January 2024, thanks to the quintile aspect between Mars and Neptune on January 22nd. This aspect fuels your wanderlust and desire for exploration. You may feel inspired to embark on a journey that allows you to broaden your horizons, expand your knowledge, and experience new cultures. Consider planning a trip to a destination that resonates with your interests and curiosity.

When traveling, make sure to prioritize self-care and well-being. Pay attention to your physical and emotional needs during your journey. Allow yourself to immerse in the experiences, savoring the sights, sounds, and tastes of new surroundings. This period may also present opportunities for spiritual growth and self-discovery. Engage in activities that promote self-reflection, such as journaling, meditation, or connecting with nature.

Additionally, if traveling isn't feasible during this time, you can explore local opportunities for cultural experiences and new adventures. Seek out events, workshops, or activities in your community that expand your horizons and offer a fresh perspective.

Remember to approach travel with an open mind and a willingness to embrace the unknown. Allow the journey to unfold naturally, and be open to the lessons and experiences that come your way. Traveling can be transformative, providing valuable insights and broadening your perspective on life.

Insight from the stars

"True love requires understanding, compromise, and unconditional acceptance. Nurture your relationships with patience and compassion."

Best days of the month: January 9th, 12th, 19th, 23rd, 28th, and 30th.

February 2024

Horoscope

Dear Pisces, in February 2024, the celestial energies bring a mix of opportunities and introspection. This month presents a powerful blend of transformative aspects, urging you to dive deep into self-reflection and embrace the potential for growth.

The month begins with Mars forming a semi-square with Saturn on February 2nd. This aspect may create a sense of frustration or tension in your ambitions and drive. It's essential to channel your energy constructively and find healthy outlets for any feelings of restlessness.

On February 5th, the Sun and Venus interact with Chiron, indicating a need for emotional healing and self-care in your relationships. Take time to address any wounds or conflicts, fostering a sense of harmony and understanding.

Mercury's conjunction with Pluto on February 5th amplifies your communication skills and empowers you with deep insights. You possess the ability to uncover hidden truths and transform your thinking patterns during this time.

The interaction between Jupiter and Saturn on February 6th emphasizes the importance of balance and long-term planning. Harness this energy to create a solid foundation for your future endeavors.

Throughout the month, Venus forms beneficial aspects with Neptune, Uranus, and Jupiter, enhancing your creativity, intuition, and romantic connections. Embrace your artistic inclinations and allow your imagination to soar. Trust your instincts in matters of the heart and explore new possibilities in your relationships.

Love

In matters of the heart, February 2024 holds potential for deep emotional connections and healing. The square aspect between Venus and Chiron on February 5th may bring up past wounds or relationship challenges. However, the Sun's sextile with Chiron on the same day offers opportunities for growth and resolution.

The Venus sextile with Uranus on February 7th introduces excitement and spontaneity into your love life. Embrace new experiences and be open to unexpected connections. This energy may also encourage you to break free from old patterns and explore different approaches to relationships.

For those already in committed partnerships, the Venus sextile with True Node on February 29th brings harmony and a sense of destiny to your connection. Trust in the path you are walking together and celebrate the journey.

Career

In terms of your career, February 2024 presents opportunities for growth and advancement. The sextile aspect between Mars and Neptune on February 7th enhances your creativity and intuition, enabling you to bring fresh perspectives and innovative ideas to your work. Trust your instincts and tap into your imaginative capabilities.

The quintile aspect between Mercury and Jupiter on February 22nd enhances your communication skills and expands your intellectual horizons. It's a favorable time for networking, learning, and exploring new professional opportunities. Embrace collaboration and seek out mentors or advisors who can support your career growth.

Finance

Financially, February 2024 encourages you to be cautious and diligent in your monetary matters. The semi-square aspect between Venus and Saturn on February 10th reminds you to be responsible and practical in your financial decisions. Avoid impulsive spending and focus on long-term stability.

The sextile between Venus and Neptune on February 13th opens up opportunities for financial gains through creative endeavors or intuitive investments. Trust your instincts and consider unconventional approaches to enhance your financial situation.

Health

Your well-being takes center stage in February 2024. The Sun's conjunction with Mercury on February 28th empowers you with mental clarity and the ability to communicate your needs effectively. Take advantage of this energy to express your emotions and seek support when necessary.

The semi-square between Mars and Neptune on February 28th reminds you to find a healthy balance between productivity and self-care. Avoid overexertion and listen to your body's signals for rest and rejuvenation.

Nurturing your emotional well-being is crucial this month. Engage in activities that promote relaxation and inner peace. Consider meditation, yoga, or therapy to address any emotional imbalances and cultivate a sense of harmony within yourself.

Travel

February 2024 offers opportunities for travel and exploration. While physical travel may vary depending on external circumstances, you can still engage in virtual or local adventures that broaden your horizons.

The semi-square between Mars and Neptune on February 24th encourages you to seek inspiration and tap into your sense of wonder. Engage in spiritual retreats, visit sacred places, or explore new cultures through books, movies, or online platforms.

Allow yourself to step out of your comfort zone and embrace the unknown. Adventure awaits, and through travel, whether physical or metaphorical, you can gain valuable insights and experiences.

Insight from the stars

"Embrace the transformative energy within you. Dive deep into self-reflection, and you shall emerge stronger and wiser. Trust your instincts, nurture your well-being, and foster harmonious relationships. Remember, the stars guide you, but it is you who shapes your destiny."

Best days of the month: February 6th, 7th, 13th, 22nd, 24th, 28th, and 29th.

March 2024

Horoscope

Dear Pisces, in March 2024, the cosmic energies invite you to embrace your intuitive and compassionate nature. This month holds transformative aspects that will awaken your spiritual awareness and deepen your connection with the world around you.

The month begins with the Sun forming a sextile with Jupiter on March 1st, bringing opportunities for growth, abundance, and self-expression. It's a favorable time to pursue your dreams and expand your horizons. Trust in your abilities and allow your optimism to guide you.

Mercury's semi-sextile with Mars on March 1st enhances your communication skills and intellectual pursuits. Your ideas and insights will have a strong impact on others, so use this energy to express yourself assertively and with clarity.

Venus forms a sextile with Chiron on March 1st, fostering healing and harmony in your relationships. Embrace vulnerability and open yourself up to deeper connections with your loved ones. It's a time for forgiveness and understanding.

Love

In matters of the heart, March 2024 offers opportunities for deep emotional connections and spiritual growth. The semi-sextile aspect between Venus and Chiron on March 26th fosters healing and compassion in your relationships. Be open to vulnerability and allow yourself to be seen and understood by your loved ones.

The sextile between Venus and Uranus on March 28th brings excitement and spontaneity to your love life. Embrace new experiences and allow your relationships to evolve naturally. Trust the journey and welcome the unexpected.

For those in committed partnerships, the conjunction between Venus and Saturn on March 21st emphasizes the importance of commitment and loyalty. Use this energy to strengthen the foundation of your relationship and establish long-term goals together.

For single Pisces individuals, this is a favorable time to explore new connections and allow your intuition to guide you. Trust your instincts and be open to the unexpected.

Career

In terms of your career, March 2024 holds the potential for professional growth and success. The semi-square between Mercury and Mars on March 14th encourages you to take assertive action and assert your ideas confidently. Trust your instincts and step into positions of leadership.

The conjunction between Venus and Saturn on March 21st brings a sense of stability and discipline to your career endeavors. This aspect highlights the importance of structure and long-term planning. Use this energy to set clear goals and work diligently toward them.

Finance

Financially, March 2024 encourages you to be cautious and strategic in your money matters. Venus' conjunction with Saturn on March 21st emphasizes the importance of long-term financial planning and stability. This is a favorable time to assess your financial goals and make practical decisions to secure your future.

The semi-sextile between Venus and Pluto on March 25th reminds you to maintain a healthy balance between material possessions and your inner sense of worth. Avoid getting caught up in external validations and focus on your intrinsic value.

Health

Your well-being takes center stage in March 2024. The Sun's conjunction with Neptune on March 17th enhances your intuition and spiritual connection, providing a sense of inner peace and harmony. Engage in practices such as meditation, yoga, or creative self-expression to nurture your soul.

Take care of your physical health by listening to your body's needs and maintaining a balanced lifestyle. Prioritize self-care and ensure you have enough rest and relaxation. Seek solace in nature and surround yourself with positive energy.

Travel

March 2024 offers opportunities for spiritual and transformative travel experiences. While physical travel may vary depending on external circumstances, you can still embark on journeys of the mind and soul.

The semi-sextile between Mars and Neptune on March 19th encourages you to seek spiritual retreats, visit sacred places, or engage in activities that uplift your soul. Allow yourself to connect with different cultures, beliefs, and perspectives.

Immerse yourself in spiritual practices or engage in self-reflection while exploring new environments, whether physically or metaphorically. Through travel, you can expand your consciousness and gain a deeper understanding of yourself and the world around you.

Insight from the stars

Remember, you have the power to manifest your dreams. Believe in yourself, trust the journey, and let your inner light guide the way.

Best days of the month: March 1st, 9th, 17th, 18th, 19th, 21st, and 25th

April 2024

Horoscope

Dear Pisces, April 2024 is a month filled with diverse energies that will have a significant impact on various aspects of your life. As a Pisces, you are naturally attuned to the ebb and flow of emotions and intuition, and this month will test your ability to navigate through these energies while maintaining balance and stability.

The month begins with Mercury in Aries forming a semi-sextile with Venus in Pisces. This alignment encourages open communication and fosters harmonious relationships. It's a great time to express your feelings and connect with loved ones on a deeper level. Use this opportunity to strengthen your emotional bonds and resolve any lingering conflicts.

The Sun in Aries also forms a semi-sextile with Saturn in Pisces, bringing a sense of discipline and structure to your life. You may feel motivated to set realistic goals and work diligently towards achieving them. This alignment highlights the importance of

50

taking responsibility for your actions and making practical decisions that will positively impact your future.

On April 3rd, the Sun forms a quintile with Pluto, amplifying your personal power and inner transformation. This aspect empowers you to tap into your hidden strengths and make significant changes in your life. It's a time for self-discovery and embracing your true potential. Trust your instincts and embrace the opportunities that come your way.

Mars also forms a quintile with Uranus on the same day, infusing you with a burst of creativity and innovation. You may find yourself drawn to unique projects or activities that allow you to express your individuality. Embrace your creative impulses and let your imagination soar.

The most significant alignment for your sign occurs on April 10th when Mars conjuncts Saturn in Pisces. This powerful conjunction brings a mix of energy and discipline to your career and ambitions. It's a time to take practical steps towards your goals and push through any obstacles that come your way. With determination and perseverance, you can make significant progress in your professional endeavors.

Love

In matters of the heart, April 2024 brings a blend of romance, emotional depth, and spiritual connections for Pisces. The Venus-Neptune conjunction on April 3rd creates a dreamy and enchanting atmosphere, enhancing your ability to connect with your partner on a profound level. This alignment inspires unconditional love, compassion, and understanding. It's a time to deepen your emotional bonds and express your affection in meaningful ways.

For single Pisces, this alignment can bring soulful and transformative connections. You may encounter someone who understands and appreciates your unique qualities. Be open to new experiences and trust your intuition when it comes to matters of the heart. Embrace vulnerability and allow yourself to be swept away by the magic of love.

The Sun's conjunction with Chiron on April 8th brings opportunities for healing and growth within your relationships. It's a time to address any emotional wounds or past traumas that may be affecting your love life. Engage in open and honest communication with your partner, and work together to heal and strengthen your bond. Embrace forgiveness and compassion, allowing your relationship to evolve into a deeper and more meaningful connection.

The Venus-Pluto sextile on April 6th intensifies your passion and desire. This alignment encourages you to explore your deepest desires and embrace the transformative power of love. It's a time to embrace intimacy and deepen your emotional and physical connections.

Career

The Mars-Saturn conjunction on April 10th emphasizes hard work and dedication. You'll need to channel your energy into focused efforts to achieve your professional goals. This alignment encourages you to embrace responsibility and take on challenging tasks with determination. Your ability to persevere through obstacles will earn you respect and recognition from your superiors.

The Sun's semi-sextile with Jupiter on April 8th brings opportunities for growth and expansion. You may receive new job offers, promotions, or invitations to collaborate on exciting projects. This alignment favors taking calculated risks and exploring new avenues in your career. Trust your instincts and have faith in your abilities.

Finance

The Venus-Neptune conjunction on April 3rd can create a dreamy and idealistic approach towards money matters. It's important to maintain a realistic perspective and avoid impulsive spending or risky financial decisions. Be cautious and rely on practical advice when it comes to managing your finances.

The Sun's semi-square with Saturn on April 20th brings a need for financial discipline and responsibility. It's a time to reassess your budget, prioritize your expenses, and make wise choices regarding investments. Avoid unnecessary expenditures and focus on long-term financial stability.

Health

Your health and well-being require special attention in April 2024, Pisces. The Mars-Saturn conjunction on April 10th may bring physical and mental exhaustion. Take breaks, prioritize self-care, and ensure you're getting enough rest to recharge your energy. Incorporating relaxation techniques such as meditation or yoga can help you maintain balance and alleviate stress.

The Sun's conjunction with Chiron on April 8th highlights the importance of addressing any lingering health issues or emotional wounds. Seek proper medical attention and take proactive steps towards healing. This alignment also emphasizes the mind-body connection, so focus on holistic approaches to wellness.

Travel

Travel may not be the primary focus for Pisces in April 2024, but there are still favorable opportunities for exploration and adventure. The Mars-Jupiter sextile on April 19th ignites your sense of wanderlust and encourages you to seek new experiences. Whether it's a short getaway or a spontaneous road trip, embrace the opportunity to broaden your horizons and immerse yourself in different cultures.

Insight from the stars

Remember, the journey is as important as the destination. Embrace the lessons, embrace the beauty, and embrace the magic of your unique existence.

Best days of the month: April 3rd, 8th, 10th, 19th, 20th and 22nd.

May 2024

Horoscope

Dear Pisces, get ready for a month of transformative energy and powerful shifts in May 2024. The planetary alignments will ignite your intuition, inspire personal growth, and bring about significant changes in various aspects of your life. It's a time to embrace your inner wisdom, trust the journey, and open yourself up to new possibilities.

May begins with Venus square Pluto on May 1st, intensifying your emotions and highlighting power dynamics in relationships. This aspect encourages you to reflect on your own desires and establish healthy boundaries. It's essential to communicate openly and honestly to foster understanding and harmony.

On May 6th, Mercury aligns with Chiron in Aries, offering opportunities for healing and self-expression. Embrace the power of your words and engage in heartfelt conversations. This alignment also encourages self-reflection and allows you to tap into your spiritual and intuitive abilities.

The Sun's sextile with Saturn on May 7th brings stability and practicality to your life. It's a favorable time for setting clear goals, organizing your responsibilities, and committing to disciplined action. This alignment supports your professional endeavors and helps you build a solid foundation for success.

Love

In matters of the heart, May 2024 brings dynamic and transformative experiences for Pisces. The Venus-Jupiter conjunction on May 23rd ignites passion, expands your romantic opportunities, and encourages you to embrace the joy of love. This alignment may bring about exciting encounters and deepen existing connections.

For single Pisces, this alignment can usher in a period of heightened attraction and magnetic energy. Embrace the possibilities that arise and be open to new romantic experiences. Trust your instincts and follow your heart's desires.

For those in committed relationships, the Venus-Jupiter conjunction brings harmony and joy. It's a time to celebrate love and appreciate the beauty of your partnership. Plan romantic getaways or indulge in activities that deepen your emotional bond.

Career

Your career takes center stage in May 2024, Pisces. The Mars-Saturn semi-sextile on May 24th emphasizes the importance of discipline, perseverance, and strategic planning. This alignment calls for a focused and structured approach to your professional endeavors. By staying dedicated and putting in consistent effort, you can overcome obstacles and achieve your goals.

The Sun's trine with Pluto on May 22nd empowers you with personal transformation and empowerment in your career. It's a time to tap into your hidden strengths and embrace new opportunities. Trust your instincts and follow your passions. Take calculated risks and step out of your comfort zone. This alignment can bring favorable advancements and recognition.

Finance

In terms of finances, May 2024 requires careful attention and wise decision-making for Pisces. The Venus-Pluto square on May 1st may bring financial complexities and power struggles. It's crucial to maintain financial stability by focusing on budgeting, avoiding unnecessary expenses, and seeking expert advice when needed.

The Sun's semi-square with Neptune on May 3rd highlights the need for clarity and discernment in financial matters. Be cautious when making investments or entering into financial agreements. Take the time to gather all the necessary information and consider the long-term implications.

Health

Your well-being and self-care are of utmost importance in May 2024, Pisces. The Sun's semi-square with Chiron on May 27th encourages you to prioritize your mental and emotional health. It's essential to take breaks, practice self-care rituals, and seek support when needed. Engaging in activities that nourish your soul, such as meditation, journaling, or spending time in nature, will enhance your overall well-being.

Pay attention to your energy levels and establish a balanced routine that allows for rest and rejuvenation. Nurturing your body and mind will enable you to navigate the transformative energies of the month with grace and resilience.

Travel

May 2024 presents opportunities for travel and exploration for Pisces. The Venus-Uranus conjunction on May 18th brings unexpected and exciting experiences in your travels. It's a time to be open to new destinations and embrace the thrill of spontaneity. Whether it's a short getaway or an extended trip, allow yourself to immerse in new cultures, expand your horizons, and create lasting memories.

Additionally, the Mars-Saturn semi-sextile on May 24th supports travel for professional purposes. If you have business or work-related travel plans, this alignment provides stability and focus. It's a favorable time for networking, attending conferences, or exploring opportunities in new locations.

Insight from the stars

"Embrace the unknown and trust your intuition. The universe has a way of guiding you towards your true path."

Best days of the month: May 7th, 13th, 18th, 22nd and 23rd.

June 2024

Horoscope

In June 2024, Pisces, the cosmic energies align to support your personal growth and inner exploration. This month presents opportunities for self-discovery, emotional healing, and expanding your horizons. The Sun's alignment with Jupiter amplifies your optimism and encourages you to dream big. It's a time to tap into your intuition, trust your instincts, and set ambitious goals. However, the presence of Venus square Saturn reminds you to maintain a practical approach and ensure a balance between your dreams and responsibilities. By combining your imaginative nature with grounded action, you can manifest your desires and achieve long-term success.

June is a month of self-reflection and introspection for Pisces. The harmonious alignment of the Sun and Neptune heightens your spiritual awareness and deepens your connection with the unseen realms. You may feel drawn to meditation, contemplation, and exploring metaphysical practices that nourish your soul. This inward focus allows you to gain clarity about your purpose and align your actions with your higher self.

Love

In matters of the heart, June brings a depth of emotional connection for Pisces. The alignment of Venus and Mars ignites passion, intensifies romantic encounters, and deepens existing relationships. It's a month of heightened sensitivity and heightened intuition in matters of love. Single Pisces may attract potential partners who appreciate their emotional depth and vulnerability. However, the square between Venus and Saturn reminds you to proceed with caution and avoid rushing into commitments. Take the time to discern true compatibility and ensure that your emotional needs align with your partner's. Communicate openly, express your feelings, and establish healthy boundaries. Nurturing self-love and self-care is also crucial during this time, as it sets the foundation for nurturing and harmonious relationships.

For those already in relationships, June offers an opportunity to strengthen the bond through deep emotional connection and understanding. Engage in heartfelt conversations, express your appreciation, and be receptive to your partner's needs. It's important to create a safe space for open and honest communication, allowing for growth and mutual support. Nurture the emotional aspects of your relationship and prioritize quality time together. Remember that love requires both passion and commitment, and with conscious effort, you can cultivate a lasting and fulfilling romantic connection.

Career

Career-wise, June presents opportunities for growth and recognition for Pisces. The alignment of the Sun with Jupiter expands your professional horizons and invites abundance into your work life. This is an excellent time to showcase your skills, take on new responsibilities, and pursue your goals with confidence. Network with colleagues, seek guidance from mentors, and explore avenues that align with your passions. Embrace new challenges and step out of your comfort zone to demonstrate your capabilities. By combining your intuitive abilities with practicality, you can make significant strides in your career. However, it's important to remain focused and disciplined in your work approach. Avoid scattering your energy or taking on too many commitments. Set clear goals, prioritize tasks, and maintain a healthy work-life balance. Remember to celebrate your achievements along the way and nurture a positive mindset.

Finance

June brings a need for financial prudence and responsible decision-making for Pisces. The square between Venus and Saturn emphasizes the importance of budgeting, long-term planning, and making informed financial choices. It's crucial to assess your financial situation, prioritize expenses, and avoid impulsive spending. This is a favorable time for reviewing your financial goals, seeking professional advice if needed, and establishing a solid foundation for future prosperity. Consider implementing strategies for saving and investing, and be mindful of your spending habits. Avoid comparing yourself to others and focus on your own financial journey. With discipline and a practical approach, you can create a stable and secure financial future. Remember that financial well-being is not solely about accumulating wealth but also about finding a balance between material comfort and emotional fulfillment.

Health

In terms of health and well-being, June encourages Pisces to prioritize self-care and holistic wellness practices. The alignment of the Sun with Neptune heightens your sensitivity, making it essential to maintain healthy boundaries and protect your energy. Nurture your emotional well-being by engaging in activities that bring you joy and relaxation. This is a favorable time for exploring mindfulness techniques, meditation, and gentle physical exercises like yoga or swimming. Pay attention to your intuition and listen to your body's signals. Rest and rejuvenate when needed, as proper rest is crucial for maintaining your overall well-being. Be mindful of emotional stressors and seek healthy outlets for processing and releasing any accumulated tension. Connecting with nature and spending time near water can be particularly therapeutic for Pisces during this period. Remember that taking care of your mental and emotional health is just as important as attending to your physical well-being.

Travel

Travel holds transformative potential for Pisces in June. Whether it's a physical trip or a metaphorical adventure of self-discovery, embrace the transformative power of travel. The alignment of Mercury and Uranus encourages spontaneity, intellectual curiosity, and expanding your perspectives. Engage in conversations with people from diverse backgrounds, immerse yourself in new cultures, and broaden your understanding of the world. Traveling can offer valuable insights, inspiration, and personal growth. If physical travel is not possible, explore new intellectual or spiritual territories through books, courses, or online communities. The key is to remain open-minded and receptive to the lessons and experiences that travel, in its various forms, brings into your life.

Insight from the stars

"Balance ambition with compassion, for true success lies in making a positive impact."

Best days of the month: June 2nd, 6th, 11th, 13th, 17th, 22nd, 29th.

July 2024

Horoscope

Dear Pisces, July brings a mix of transformative energies and opportunities for self-reflection. The alignment of Jupiter and Chiron at the beginning of the month encourages deep healing and growth. It's a time to address emotional wounds, release old patterns, and embrace a newfound sense of self-awareness. This process may require courage and vulnerability, but the rewards will be profound. Trust the journey and allow yourself to embrace the transformation that awaits.

The Sun's square with Uranus on July 1st may bring unexpected shifts and disruptions in your daily routine. Remain flexible and adaptable as you navigate these changes, as they may ultimately lead you towards new and exciting possibilities. Embrace the element of surprise and trust that the universe is guiding you towards your highest good.

Love

In matters of the heart, July offers opportunities for deepening emotional connections and fostering greater intimacy. The trine between Venus and Saturn on July 2nd creates a stable and harmonious energy in your relationships. It's a time to cultivate trust, commitment, and loyalty with your partner. Single Pisces may attract a potential long-term partner who shares their values and desires for a committed relationship.

However, the opposition between Venus and Pluto on July 12th may bring some intensity and power struggles in relationships. It's important to maintain open and honest communication, addressing any underlying issues that may arise. Use this time to deepen your emotional bonds and explore the depths of your connections.

Career

July presents promising opportunities for career advancement and professional growth for Pisces. The alignment of Mercury trine Neptune on July 2nd enhances your intuition and creativity, making it an excellent time for innovative thinking and problem-solving. Use this heightened mental clarity to pursue your professional goals with enthusiasm and determination. The sextile between Mercury and

Jupiter on July 8th amplifies your communication skills, making it an ideal time for networking, negotiations, and collaboration. Embrace this energy to expand your professional connections and seek new opportunities for growth. However, be cautious of the influence of the sesquiquadrate aspect between Mercury and Pluto on July 14th, which may bring power struggles or hidden agendas in your work environment. Maintain integrity and diplomacy when dealing with challenging situations. Overall, July encourages you to take calculated risks, trust in your abilities, and make proactive choices that align with your long-term career aspirations.

Finance

July brings a favorable financial outlook for Pisces, with opportunities for stability and abundance. The trine between Venus and Saturn on July 2nd supports your financial endeavors, bringing practicality and discipline to your money management. This alignment encourages responsible spending and long-term financial planning. Consider seeking advice from a financial expert to ensure wise investments and effective strategies for wealth accumulation. Be cautious of impulsive spending and prioritize financial security. The influence of the biquintile aspect between Mercury and Saturn on July 10th further enhances your financial acumen, enabling you to make sound decisions and find innovative solutions to enhance your financial well-being. Remember to balance practicality with your creative pursuits, allowing yourself to enjoy the fruits of your labor while maintaining financial stability.

Health

In terms of health and well-being, July urges Pisces to prioritize self-care and maintain a balanced lifestyle. The semi-square between the Sun and Jupiter on July 18th may bring a tendency to overindulge or neglect healthy habits. Practice moderation and self-discipline to avoid any potential negative consequences. The trine between the Sun and Neptune on July 21st supports your emotional and spiritual well-being. Engage in activities that nurture your soul, such as meditation, journaling, or spending time in nature. Embrace your creative side and explore artistic outlets to find solace and inspiration. Be mindful of your physical health by maintaining a balanced diet, engaging in regular exercise, and getting sufficient rest. Listen to your body's needs and practice self-care rituals that rejuvenate and energize you.

Travel

July offers exciting prospects for travel and exploration for Pisces. The square between Mercury and Uranus on July 21st encourages spontaneity and intellectual stimulation. Embrace opportunities to broaden your horizons through physical travel or immersing yourself in new cultures and experiences. Travel can provide valuable insights, broaden your perspectives, and inspire personal growth. If physical travel is not feasible, consider exploring new intellectual territories through books, courses, or online communities. Embrace a sense of curiosity and remain open to the lessons and experiences that travel, in its various forms, brings into your life. Remember to prioritize your safety and well-being while traveling and be open to the unexpected, as it may lead to transformative experiences and new connections.

Insight from the stars

"Remember, you are a divine being with infinite potential. Trust in your journey and believe in your own magic."

Best days of the month: July 2nd, 8th, 15th, 18th, 21st, 23rd and 30th

August 2024

Horoscope

Dear Pisces, welcome to the transformative month of August! The celestial alignments bring a dynamic and powerful energy into your life, encouraging personal growth and self-discovery. This month is a time of great significance for you as you navigate through various aspects of your life, including love, career, finances, health, and travel.

The planetary movements highlight the importance of balance and self-care. It is crucial for you to prioritize your well-being during this period of growth and change. Take the time to reflect on your emotions, desires, and aspirations, as this will enable you to make conscious decisions and align yourself with your true purpose.

The square between Venus in Leo and Uranus in Taurus on August 2nd may bring unexpected shifts or disruptions in your relationships. This alignment could manifest as sudden changes in your love life or an urge for freedom and independence. It is important to be open to adaptability and embrace compromise, as this can lead to new understandings and growth within your partnerships. Allow yourself and your partner the space to express individuality while maintaining the connection you share.

In summary, August holds immense potential for your personal and spiritual growth, Pisces. Embrace the transformative energies and embrace the opportunities that come your way. Remember to maintain balance, prioritize self-care, and listen to your intuition. By doing so, you will navigate this month with grace and emerge stronger and wiser.

Love

In matters of the heart, August presents both challenges and opportunities for Pisces. The square between Venus in Leo and Uranus in Taurus on August 2nd may bring unexpected shifts or disruptions in your relationships. This could manifest as sudden changes in your love life or an urge for freedom and independence. It's crucial to be open to adaptability and embrace compromise, as this can lead to new understandings and growth within your partnerships. Allow yourself and your partner the space to express individuality while maintaining the connection you share.

On August 10th, the biquintile aspect between Venus and Pluto amplifies the intensity of passion and deep emotional connections. This alignment encourages you to explore the depths of your emotions and forge transformative experiences in your relationships. Embrace vulnerability and honesty, as they are the foundations for fostering deeper connections with your partner.

However, be cautious of the quincunx aspect between Venus and Jupiter on August 19th. This alignment may bring challenges in finding a balance between your personal desires and the needs of your partner. It's essential to engage in open and honest communication to maintain harmony in your relationships. Remember, compromise is key, and by finding a middle ground, you can strengthen the bond you share.

Career

August brings opportunities for career advancement and professional growth for Pisces. The conjunction between Mercury and Venus on August 7th enhances your communication and networking skills, making it an ideal time for collaboration and building connections in your professional life. Your natural charm and charisma will leave a lasting impression on others, opening doors for new opportunities.

The sesquiquadrate aspect between Mercury and Pluto on August 14th may bring power struggles or challenges in the workplace. It's crucial to maintain professionalism and integrity during this time. Focus on finding practical solutions to overcome obstacles and collaborate with others to achieve your goals. By displaying resilience and adaptability, you can navigate these challenges with grace and success.

On August 14th, the conjunction between Mars and Jupiter ignites your ambition and drive for success. This powerful alignment propels you forward and encourages you to take risks, pursue new ventures, and step into leadership roles. However, it's important to strike a balance between assertiveness and diplomacy. By fostering a collaborative environment, you can inspire and motivate those around you, creating a harmonious work atmosphere.

Finance

August brings a need for careful financial planning and decision-making for Pisces. The quincunx aspect between Venus in Virgo and Neptune in Pisces on August 4th may cloud your judgment when it comes to money matters. It's crucial to take a cautious approach and seek advice from financial experts before making any major financial decisions. Be mindful of your spending habits and avoid impulsive purchases. Focus on practicality and long-term stability to ensure financial security.

The trine between Venus and Uranus on August 27th brings opportunities for financial stability and unexpected windfalls. However, it's important to exercise caution and resist the temptation to overspend. Embrace a disciplined approach to your finances, considering budgeting and saving for future endeavors. By reevaluating your financial goals and making necessary adjustments, you can align your aspirations with your monetary resources.

Health

In terms of health and well-being, August emphasizes the need for balance and self-care for Pisces. The quincunx aspect between the Sun in Leo and Neptune in Pisces on August 29th may bring a sense of confusion or lack of clarity in matters of health. It's important to listen to your body's signals and trust your instincts. Focus on maintaining a balanced diet, engaging in regular exercise, and getting sufficient rest and relaxation.

The biquintile aspect between Mercury and Neptune on August 23rd enhances your intuition and spiritual connection. This alignment encourages practices such as meditation, yoga, or journaling, which can help you find inner peace and promote overall well-being. Embrace activities that nourish your soul and provide a sense of calm and tranquility.

Remember to prioritize self-care and engage in activities that bring you joy and rejuvenation. Surround yourself with positive influences and seek support from loved ones when needed. By nurturing your physical, emotional, and spiritual health, you can navigate the month with grace and vitality.

Travel

August presents opportunities for travel and exploration for Pisces. The biquintile aspect between Mercury and Neptune on August 23rd enhances your intuition and connection to the spiritual realms. Embrace journeys that allow for personal growth and spiritual awakening. Whether it's a physical journey or an inner exploration, trust your instincts and follow your heart's guidance. Seek out destinations that resonate with your soul and offer opportunities for self-discovery. Consider visiting places known for their natural beauty, cultural richness, or spiritual significance. Engage in activities that foster creativity and provide inspiration. Be open to new cultures and perspectives, as they may offer valuable insights and deepen your understanding of the world.

Insight from the stars

"Find peace in the present moment, for it is where true happiness resides and remember, you are a co-creator of your destiny. Trust in the power within you to manifest your dreams."

Best days of the month: August 2nd, 7th, 14th, 15th, 23rd, 27th and 31st.

September 2024

Horoscope

September is a month filled with dynamic energy and significant opportunities for Pisces individuals. The celestial movements and planetary aspects indicate a period of growth, transformation, and self-discovery. It is essential for Pisces to tap into their intuitive nature, embrace change, and harness their emotional intelligence to make the most of this transformative month.

In September, Pisces individuals will experience a heightened sense of self-awareness and a deeper connection with their emotions. The month begins with Mercury forming a trine with Chiron on September 2nd, creating an atmosphere of emotional healing and introspection. This alignment encourages Pisces to engage in meaningful conversations, seek understanding, and release any emotional wounds that may be holding them back.

In summary, September is a month of immense growth, transformation, and self-discovery for Pisces individuals. By tapping into their intuition, embracing change, and maintaining a balanced approach in various areas of life, Pisces can navigate through this dynamic period successfully and emerge stronger and wiser.

Love

Love and relationships will be a central theme for Pisces in September. The month begins with Mercury forming a harmonious trine with Chiron, enhancing communication and emotional healing in partnerships. This aspect promotes open conversations and deep connections.

On September 3rd, Mars squares Neptune, creating some confusion and potential conflicts in romantic relationships. It is crucial for Pisces individuals to clarify their boundaries and avoid sacrificing their needs for the sake of harmony.

Venus opposes the True Node on September 3rd, indicating a time for reflection and reassessment in matters of love. Some Pisces may feel a need to reassess their relationship dynamics and seek a greater balance between their own desires and the needs of their partners.

As the month progresses, Venus forms a quincunx with Saturn on September 11th, highlighting the importance of commitment and responsibility in relationships. Pisces individuals may feel compelled to reassess their long-term goals and make adjustments to align with their partners.

Career

Career prospects for Pisces in September are influenced by various planetary aspects. The month begins with the Sun quintile Mars on September 2nd, fostering ambition, drive, and the ability to take assertive action in professional endeavors. This alignment boosts confidence and encourages Pisces to pursue their goals with enthusiasm.

On September 7th, Mercury squares Uranus, indicating unexpected changes and disruptions in the workplace. Pisces individuals should be prepared to adapt swiftly and think creatively to overcome any obstacles that arise.

The opposition between the Sun and Saturn on September 8th brings attention to long-term career goals. It is a time for Pisces individuals to evaluate their professional trajectory, consider their achievements, and make any necessary adjustments to ensure their work aligns with their aspirations.

Mercury's quincunx with Neptune on September 8th calls for clarity and careful communication. Pisces individuals should pay attention to detail and avoid miscommunications that could potentially impact their professional relationships.

The quintile between Mercury and Jupiter on September 10th offers opportunities for intellectual growth and expanded perspectives. Pisces individuals should seek out new knowledge, engage in networking, and consider new possibilities in their career.

.

Finance

The financial outlook for Pisces in September carries a mix of opportunities and challenges. It is crucial for Pisces individuals to exercise caution and adopt a disciplined approach to their monetary matters.

On September 15th, Venus trines Jupiter, indicating potential financial gains and opportunities. Pisces individuals should be open to exploring new investment prospects or seeking advice from financial experts to make the most of this favorable alignment.

However, Venus' opposition to Chiron on September 16th suggests the need for caution and careful evaluation of financial decisions. Pisces individuals should avoid impulsive purchases or risky ventures during this period.

The square between Venus and Pluto on September 22nd brings forth potential financial conflicts or power struggles. It is essential for Pisces individuals to prioritize open and honest communication when dealing with financial matters involving partners or business associates.

Throughout the month, Pisces individuals should maintain a balanced approach to their finances. It is advisable to create a budget, track expenses, and seek professional advice if needed. By practicing mindfulness and discipline, Pisces can navigate the financial landscape successfully.

Health

Pisces individuals should pay close attention to their physical and emotional well-being in September. The planetary aspects suggest a need for self-care and maintaining a healthy balance between mind, body, and soul.

The sesquiquadrate between the Sun and Pluto on September 6th emphasizes the importance of self-transformation and personal growth. Pisces individuals should focus on releasing any emotional baggage that may be affecting their overall well-being.

Mercury's opposition to Neptune on September 25th brings potential mental fog and confusion. It is essential for Pisces individuals to prioritize rest, relaxation, and engaging in activities that promote mental clarity and emotional balance.

Regular exercise, a balanced diet, and sufficient rest are crucial for Pisces individuals throughout September. Engaging in activities that promote spiritual well-being, such as meditation or yoga, can also contribute to maintaining overall health.

Travel

Travel opportunities arise for Pisces individuals in September, offering a chance for new experiences and personal growth. It is essential to plan trips carefully and remain adaptable to any unforeseen changes.

On September 25th, the Sun's opposition to Neptune suggests that Pisces individuals should exercise caution when traveling, ensuring they have all necessary documents and carefully following safety guidelines.

The quincunx between Venus and Neptune on September 21st may bring potential travel disruptions or unexpected changes in plans. Pisces individuals should remain flexible and have backup options in place to navigate any challenges that arise.

Whether embarking on a physical journey or exploring new horizons within themselves, Pisces individuals should embrace the spirit of adventure and remain open to the lessons and experiences that travel can bring.

Insight from the stars

"Nurture your dreams, for they are the seeds of your future. With passion and perseverance, you can turn them into reality. Also remember, dear Pisces, that self-care is not a luxury but a necessity. Take time to nourish your mind, body, and spirit."

Best days of the month: September 2nd, 15th, 19th, 21st, 22nd, 26th, 30th.

October 2024

Horoscope

October brings forth a powerful and transformative energy for Pisces individuals. With celestial movements and planetary aspects influencing their lives, this month holds the potential for growth, introspection, and profound changes. Pisces individuals are encouraged to embrace their intuition, dive deep into their emotions, and utilize their creativity to navigate this transformative period.

The month begins with Mercury forming a sesquiquadrate with Uranus on October 2nd. This alignment may bring unexpected shifts or disruptions in communication. Pisces individuals are advised to remain adaptable and open-minded to effectively navigate any challenges that arise.

Overall, October is a transformative month for Pisces individuals. By embracing their intuition, nurturing their relationships, remaining cautious with finances, prioritizing self-care, and planning their travel adventures carefully, Pisces can navigate through this period with grace and emerge stronger and wiser.

Love

Love and relationships take center stage for Pisces individuals in October. The planetary aspects indicate a period of introspection, emotional healing, and the potential for deep connections.

The semi-sextile between Mercury and Venus on October 3rd brings attention to the balance between personal desires and harmonious partnerships. Pisces individuals may find themselves contemplating their needs and how they align with their relationships. It is essential to engage in open and honest communication, expressing their desires and concerns with clarity and compassion.

On October 7th, Venus quintiles Pluto, enhancing the intensity and transformative potential of romantic connections. This alignment encourages Pisces individuals to explore the depths of their emotions and embrace vulnerability in their relationships. It is a time for profound emotional growth and increased intimacy.

However, challenges may arise on October 10th when Venus forms a quincunx with Jupiter and Chiron. Pisces individuals may feel torn between their personal desires and the expectations of their partners or societal norms. It is crucial to find a balance between individual needs and the shared goals within relationships.

The month progresses with Venus trining Neptune on October 15th, fostering deep emotional connections and spiritual alignment in partnerships. Pisces individuals may experience heightened compassion, empathy, and an intuitive understanding of their partner's needs.

Career

October brings opportunities for career advancement and growth for Pisces individuals. The planetary aspects indicate a favorable period for professional development and recognition.

The biquintile between Venus and the True Node on October 3rd suggests that Pisces individuals should trust their instincts and explore new avenues for career expansion. It is a time to align their professional goals with their authentic selves and seek opportunities that resonate with their passions.

On October 4th, Venus trines Saturn, providing stability and support in career matters. This alignment highlights the importance of discipline, dedication, and a strong work ethic. Pisces individuals may receive recognition for their hard work and find themselves in a position of authority or leadership.

However, the square between Mercury and Mars on October 6th calls for careful planning and attention to detail. Pisces individuals should avoid impulsive decisions and prioritize strategic thinking in their professional endeavors. It is important to stay focused, communicate clearly, and maintain a professional approach to achieve desired outcomes.

Throughout October, Pisces individuals should also pay attention to networking opportunities and collaborations. The biquintile between Mercury and Jupiter on October 23rd enhances intellectual growth and expands perspectives. It is a favorable time for connecting with mentors, seeking advice from experts in their field, and exploring new possibilities in their career.

By embracing their natural intuition, staying disciplined, and remaining open to new opportunities, Pisces individuals can make significant strides in their professional lives during October.

Finance

Financial matters require careful consideration and discernment for Pisces individuals in October. The planetary aspects suggest a need for caution and strategic planning.

The semi-sextile between Mercury and Uranus on October 2nd may bring unexpected financial changes or disruptions. Pisces individuals should remain adaptable and be prepared to make necessary adjustments to their budget or financial plans.

On October 3rd, Venus forms a sesquiquadrate with Neptune, highlighting the importance of clarity and discernment in financial decisions. Pisces individuals should be cautious of potential illusions or unrealistic expectations regarding financial investments. It is advisable to seek professional advice and carefully evaluate the risks before committing to any major financial ventures.

The quincunx between Mercury and Saturn on October 4th calls for responsible financial management and a disciplined approach to money matters. Pisces individuals should review their financial goals, create a realistic budget, and prioritize savings. It is crucial to avoid impulsive spending and focus on long-term stability.

Health

In October, Pisces individuals should prioritize their physical and emotional well-being. The planetary aspects suggest a need for self-care, emotional healing, and maintaining balance.

The quincunx between Mercury and Saturn on October 4th may bring mental and emotional challenges. Pisces individuals should pay attention to their stress levels and find healthy outlets to manage any feelings of overwhelm. Engaging in activities that promote relaxation, such as meditation, yoga, or spending time in nature, can be beneficial for maintaining emotional equilibrium.

The square between Mercury and Pluto on October 13th may also bring intensity and potential power struggles. It is crucial for Pisces individuals to set healthy boundaries and prioritize self-care during this period. Taking breaks, practicing self-compassion, and seeking support from loved ones or professionals can help in managing stress and emotional well-being.

Throughout October, Pisces individuals should prioritize a balanced approach to their health. Regular exercise, a nutritious diet, and sufficient rest are essential for maintaining physical vitality. Additionally, focusing on emotional healing, such as therapy or journaling, can aid in overall well-being and inner harmony.

Travel

Travel opportunities arise for Pisces individuals in October, offering a chance for new experiences and personal growth. The planetary aspects suggest the need for careful planning and adaptability.

The square between Mercury and Mars on October 6th calls for attention to detail and strategic thinking in travel plans. Pisces individuals should ensure they have all necessary documents, make arrangements in advance, and remain flexible to handle any unexpected changes or challenges that may arise during their journeys.

On October 14th, Venus opposes Uranus, which may bring some disruptions or unexpected events during travel. Pisces individuals should be prepared for potential changes in itineraries or delays. Flexibility and a positive mindset will help navigate through any travel-related challenges.

Throughout October, Pisces individuals should approach travel with an open mind and a spirit of adventure. Embracing new cultures, exploring unfamiliar territories, and engaging in meaningful experiences can contribute to personal growth and transformation.

By planning ahead, staying adaptable, and embracing the journey, Pisces individuals can make the most of their travel experiences in October.

Insight from the stars

"Trust the ebb and flow of your emotions, dear Pisces, for within them lie the secrets of your soul's journey and in matters of the heart, listen to the whispers of intuition, for they hold the key to profound connections and authentic love."

Best days of the month: October 8th, 12th, 15th, 21st, 22nd, 28th and 31st.

November 2024

Horoscope

November brings a dynamic and transformative energy for Pisces individuals. The planetary aspects indicate a period of introspection, growth, and potential breakthroughs in various areas of life.

The sextile between Jupiter and Chiron on November 2nd sets the tone for self-discovery and healing. Pisces individuals are encouraged to explore their inner depths, confront emotional wounds, and embrace personal growth. This alignment provides an opportunity for profound spiritual and emotional transformation.

On November 4th, the Sun forms a sesquiquadrate with Neptune, urging Pisces individuals to balance their dreams and ideals with practicality. It is important to stay grounded and realistic while pursuing their aspirations. Seeking guidance from mentors or trusted individuals can provide valuable insights during this period.

Throughout November, the trine between the Sun and Saturn on November 4th offers stability and support in various areas of life. This alignment enhances discipline, responsibility, and a methodical approach to achieving long-term goals. Pisces individuals can make significant progress by staying focused, organized, and committed to their endeavors.

Overall, November is a transformative month for Pisces individuals. By embracing self-reflection, maintaining balance, and remaining open to new experiences, they can make significant strides in personal growth, relationships, career, and overall well-being.

Love

In November, Pisces individuals may experience profound shifts and growth in their love life. The planetary aspects indicate a period of self-discovery, emotional healing, and transformative relationships.

The opposition between Venus and Jupiter on November 3rd brings a need for balance in romantic relationships. Pisces individuals may find themselves torn between their personal desires and the expectations of their partners. It is essential to engage in open and honest communication, express needs and boundaries, and find a compromise that nurtures both individuals' growth.

The trine between Venus and Chiron on November 3rd signifies an opportunity for emotional healing and deep connection in partnerships. Pisces individuals may experience a profound understanding of their own vulnerabilities and those of their partners. By embracing empathy, compassion, and active listening, they can foster relationships that support personal growth and mutual healing.

Throughout November, Pisces individuals are encouraged to embark on a journey of self-love and self-acceptance. The sextile between Mercury and Mars on November 2nd enhances communication skills, enabling them to express their needs and desires with confidence. By embracing their authentic selves, they can attract and cultivate relationships that align with their true values and aspirations.

For Pisces individuals in committed relationships, the trine between Venus and Saturn on November 22nd provides stability and support. This alignment fosters commitment, loyalty, and a sense of shared responsibility. It is a favorable time to strengthen bonds, deepen trust, and work towards long-term goals as a couple.

Career

November brings significant opportunities for career growth and advancement for Pisces individuals. The planetary aspects indicate a period of increased focus, assertiveness, and strategic thinking.

The sextile between Mercury and Mars on November 2nd enhances communication skills and assertiveness in the workplace. Pisces individuals will find themselves adept at expressing their ideas, asserting their opinions, and initiating productive collaborations. This alignment empowers them to take decisive actions and make significant progress in their professional endeavors.

Throughout November, Pisces individuals are encouraged to embrace their creative abilities and innovative thinking. The opposition between Mercury and Jupiter on November 18th stimulates intellectual curiosity and expansion of knowledge. Engaging in learning opportunities, seeking new perspectives, and being open to unconventional ideas will contribute to their professional growth and success.

The trine between the Sun and Saturn on November 4th offers stability and support in career matters. Pisces individuals are likely to experience recognition for their hard work, dedication, and discipline. This alignment encourages them to focus on long-term goals, maintain a methodical approach, and take on leadership roles with confidence.

The square between Venus and Neptune on November 9th calls for discernment and clarity in financial matters. Pisces individuals should exercise caution when it comes to financial decisions, investments, or collaborations. Seeking advice from trusted financial advisors and conducting thorough research will help navigate potential risks and ensure stability.

Finance

November brings a focus on financial matters for Pisces individuals. The planetary aspects indicate a need for discernment, practicality, and strategic planning in managing their finances.

The square between Venus and Neptune on November 9th calls for caution and clarity in financial decisions. Pisces individuals should avoid impulsive spending or making investments without thorough research. It is essential to seek advice from trusted financial advisors and maintain a realistic approach to their financial goals.

Throughout November, Pisces individuals are encouraged to review their budget and identify areas where they can save or cut back on expenses. The opposition between Mercury and Jupiter on November 18th stimulates intellectual curiosity and expansion of knowledge. Engaging in financial literacy courses or seeking guidance from financial experts can contribute to their financial growth and stability.

The trine between Venus and Saturn on November 22nd offers stability and support in financial matters. This alignment enhances discipline, responsible financial management, and a methodical approach to achieving long-term financial goals. Pisces individuals are encouraged to stay focused, organized, and committed to their financial plans.

It is also important for Pisces individuals to cultivate an abundance mindset and embrace opportunities for financial growth. By leveraging their creativity, intuition, and unique skills, they can attract prosperity and explore new avenues for generating income.

Health

November brings a focus on physical and emotional well-being for Pisces individuals. The planetary aspects indicate a need for self-care, stress management, and a balanced approach to health.

The opposition between the Sun and Uranus on November 16th may bring unexpected disruptions or changes in health routines. Pisces individuals should prioritize self-care, listen to their bodies' needs, and be adaptable in adjusting their wellness practices. Incorporating mindfulness techniques, such as meditation or yoga, can help maintain emotional balance during periods of uncertainty.

Throughout November, it is important for Pisces individuals to manage stress levels effectively. Engaging in stress-reducing activities, such as exercise, spending time in nature, or pursuing creative outlets, will contribute to their overall well-being. Maintaining a healthy work-life balance and setting boundaries in personal and professional life is crucial for managing stress.

The trine between the Sun and Neptune on November 18th offers an opportunity for spiritual and emotional rejuvenation. Pisces individuals can tap into their intuitive and compassionate nature to support their mental and emotional well-being. Exploring practices such as meditation, journaling, or seeking therapy can enhance self-awareness and provide emotional healing.

Maintaining a nutritious diet and regular exercise routine is vital for Pisces individuals in November. Nurturing their bodies with wholesome foods and engaging in physical activities that they enjoy will promote vitality and overall health. It is advisable to consult with healthcare professionals or nutritionists to personalize their diet and exercise regimen.

Travel

November presents opportunities for travel and exploration for Pisces individuals. The planetary aspects indicate a desire for adventure, cultural experiences, and broadening horizons.

The sextile between Venus and Saturn on November 22nd brings favorable energy for travel. Pisces individuals can embark on new adventures, explore different cultures, and expand their horizons. Planning ahead and remaining open to unexpected opportunities will make travel experiences memorable and fulfilling.

During November, Pisces individuals are encouraged to engage in mindful and immersive travel experiences. The opposition between Mercury and Jupiter on November 18th stimulates intellectual curiosity and expansion of knowledge. Exploring historical sites, engaging in local traditions, or seeking out educational opportunities while traveling will enhance their overall experience and personal growth.

It is advisable for Pisces individuals to prioritize self-care and maintain their well-being while traveling. Ensuring sufficient rest, staying hydrated, and being mindful of their physical and emotional needs will contribute to a positive and fulfilling travel experience.

Pisces individuals may also find value in connecting with local communities or engaging in volunteer work during their travels. By immersing themselves in the culture and giving back to the communities they visit, they can forge meaningful connections and make a positive impact.

Insight from the stars

"Communication is the key to harmonious relationships. Express your needs, listen attentively, and find a compromise that nurtures both your growth and that of your loved ones."

Best days of the month: November 2nd, 4th, 9th, 16th, 18th 22nd and 27th.

December 2024

Horoscope

December brings a mix of challenges and opportunities for Pisces individuals. The planetary aspects indicate the need for balance, adaptability, and self-reflection. It is a month of growth, transformation, and introspection.

The opposition between the Sun and Saturn on December 4th may bring feelings of limitation or a need for discipline in various areas of life. Pisces individuals are advised to embrace responsibility, assess their long-term goals, and make necessary adjustments to achieve success.

The conjunction between the Sun and Mercury on December 5th enhances communication skills and intellectual clarity. It is an excellent time for self-expression, initiating important conversations, and sharing ideas with others.

The square aspect between Mercury and Saturn on December 6th can present challenges in communication and decision-making. Pisces individuals should exercise patience, seek advice when needed, and approach conflicts with a diplomatic mindset.

Overall, December encourages Pisces individuals to embrace responsibility, enhance communication skills, and navigate challenges with resilience and adaptability. It is a month of personal growth, transformation, and cultivating meaningful connections.

Love

In December, love and relationships take center stage for Pisces individuals. The planetary aspects indicate opportunities for deepening connections, addressing emotional needs, and fostering growth in romantic partnerships.

The conjunction between the Sun and Mercury on December 5th enhances communication and intellectual compatibility in relationships. Pisces individuals are encouraged to express their feelings, engage in meaningful conversations, and share their desires and aspirations with their partners.

The opposition between Venus and Mars on December 12th may bring some challenges in love relationships. It is essential for Pisces individuals to be patient, understanding, and open to compromise. By nurturing open communication, addressing conflicts constructively, and showing empathy, they can overcome challenges and strengthen their bonds.

The trine between Venus and Jupiter on December 19th brings harmony, optimism, and social opportunities. This aspect favors romantic encounters, deepening connections, and expanding social circles. Single Pisces individuals may attract potential partners during this period.

The semi-square between Venus and Neptune on December 17th may create moments of confusion or idealization in relationships. It is crucial for Pisces individuals to maintain realistic expectations, communicate openly, and address any emotional vulnerabilities. Honesty and clarity will contribute to the growth and stability of their romantic partnerships.

Career

December presents both challenges and opportunities in the career sector for Pisces individuals. The planetary aspects indicate the need for adaptability, resilience, and a strategic approach to career growth.

The opposition between the Sun and Saturn on December 4th may bring professional challenges or a need for disciplined efforts. Pisces individuals are advised to assess their long-term goals, enhance their skills, and make necessary adjustments to overcome obstacles and achieve success.

The square aspect between Mercury and Saturn on December 6th can create communication challenges or delays in decision-making. Pisces individuals should exercise patience, seek advice when needed, and approach conflicts with a diplomatic mindset. By maintaining professionalism and adopting a solution-oriented approach, they can overcome hurdles and make progress in their careers.

The conjunction between the Sun and Mercury on December 5th enhances communication skills and intellectual clarity. It is an excellent time for Pisces individuals to express their ideas confidently, engage in collaborative projects, and share their expertise. Networking and building relationships with colleagues and superiors can open doors for career advancement.

The trine between Venus and Jupiter on December 19th brings optimism, abundance, and opportunities for professional growth. Pisces individuals should remain open to new possibilities, take calculated risks, and seek mentorship or guidance to enhance their career prospects.

Finance

The opposition between the Sun and Saturn on December 4th may create financial challenges or a need for disciplined spending. Pisces individuals should assess their financial goals, create a budget, and exercise prudence in their expenses. Avoid impulsive purchases and prioritize long-term financial stability.

The semi-square between Venus and Saturn on December 5th may bring a need for financial restraint and responsible money management. Pisces individuals should prioritize savings, avoid unnecessary expenses, and seek professional advice when making significant financial decisions.

The trine between Venus and Jupiter on December 19th brings opportunities for financial growth and abundance. It is an excellent time to explore new avenues for income generation, invest wisely, and seek potential opportunities for financial stability.

The semi-square between Venus and Neptune on December 17th may create moments of financial confusion or idealization. Pisces individuals should maintain realistic expectations, conduct thorough research before making financial commitments, and seek advice from trusted advisors.

Health

The opposition between the Sun and Saturn on December 4th may create financial challenges or a need for disciplined spending. Pisces individuals should assess their financial goals, create a budget, and exercise prudence in their expenses. Avoid impulsive purchases and prioritize long-term financial stability.

The semi-square between Venus and Saturn on December 5th may bring a need for financial restraint and responsible money management. Pisces individuals should prioritize savings, avoid unnecessary expenses, and seek professional advice when making significant financial decisions.

The trine between Venus and Jupiter on December 19th brings opportunities for financial growth and abundance. It is an excellent time to explore new avenues for income generation, invest wisely, and seek potential opportunities for financial stability.

The semi-square between Venus and Neptune on December 17th may create moments of financial confusion or idealization. Pisces individuals should maintain realistic expectations, conduct thorough research before making financial commitments, and seek advice from trusted advisors.

Travel

In December, Pisces individuals may feel drawn to travel and exploration. The planetary aspects indicate opportunities for new experiences, cultural enrichment, and expanding horizons.

The conjunction between the Sun and Mercury on December 5th enhances communication skills, making it an excellent time for Pisces individuals to embark on travel adventures, engage with different cultures, and embrace new experiences. It is advisable to plan trips that involve intellectual stimulation, such as visiting historical sites or attending educational events.

The trine between Venus and Jupiter on December 19th brings opportunities for joyful and enriching travel experiences. Pisces individuals should consider travel destinations that align with their interests and offer opportunities for personal growth and relaxation. It is a favorable time to connect with loved ones, explore new environments, and create lasting memories.

The semi-square between Venus and Neptune on December 17th may create moments of indecision or confusion regarding travel plans. Pisces individuals should conduct thorough research, seek advice from travel experts, and trust their intuition when making travel-related decisions.

Insight from the stars

"Trust your intuition in all aspects of life. Your inner wisdom will guide you towards the path of fulfillment and happiness."

Best days of the month: December 2nd, 5th, 12th, 19th, 23rd, 24th and 31st.

Printed in Great Britain
by Amazon

34807238R00066